ANIMALS

through

the

LENS

THROUGH THE LENS

PHOTOGRAPHS
AND TEXT BY

WŁODZIMIERZ
PUCHALSKI

Abbey Library

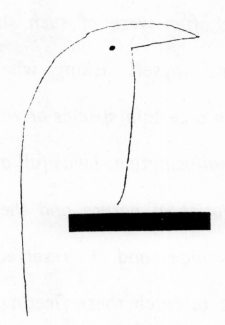

INTRODUCTION

I have travelled for many years through the various regions of our country and have become well acquainted with its rich and very varied fauna. During my travels I have had numerous very interesting encounters with the inhabitants of the large forests. Many of these encounters took place in dense undergrowth or

I

thickets and often were of such short duration that I found myself asking whether I had actually seen a certain species or whether it was merely an hallucination. I was full of admiration for the beauties of nature and the phenomena that I observed and I resolved to make every effort to catch these fleeting scenes with a camera and keep them as a lasting record. A good photograph is not only of artistic value but is a most useful scientific document. There are many people who indulge in this hobby, or as I prefer to call it "this passion," and the number of enthusiasts for the bloodless hunt increases day by day. The photographs that are taken, however, are by no means always a success.

It is a grave error to think that it suffices merely to have good equipment in order to take fine photographs. There are numerous other factors which have to be taken into account, especially where animal photography is concerned. One needs, for a start, an excellent knowledge of the animal that is to be photographed, and the ability and patience to approach the animal: only when these factors have been taken into account does good equipment and good technique start to play its part.

There are so many ways and means of approaching and photographing wild creatures in their natural habitat. The first and most important thing is to hide in such a way that the animal does not feel danger threatens at the moment when you are about to take the photograph. Sometimes it suffices to hide behind a thick tree or in tall, dense grass or merely to squat behind dense bushes and stand immobile, but often even the best hiding place will not conceal you from

the sharp eyes, sensitive nose and acute hearing

of many animals that live in the wild state.

In order to be successful in this bloodless

hunt a knowledge of the habits and typical

surroundings of the various species of animal

is an absolute necessity. If, for example,

we know that the badger is a nocturnal animal

that stays in his subterranean burrow all day,

then it is obvious that to photograph him we

will have to lie in wait near the entrance to

his burrow at night with a flashlight. When

one sets out with a camera to hunt mammalia

one should know exactly where to find the

animal runs, where the animals feed and water

and where they rest. It is obvious that in these

places you will have the best chance of finding

them. If, in addition, the animal does not get wind

of the hunter, then he can have every reason to expect a successful hunt.

With birds there is no need to fear that they may get wind of you, but they have very keen eyesight and they will quickly spot the minutest defect in a hiding place. If you know the birds' feeding grounds and hatching places you may well be able to photograph them successfully from a distance of only a few paces. This however will depend upon the quality of your hiding place. Mammals and birds are very shy and it is almost impossible to take a portrait without a telephoto lens. Reptiles and insects and amphibia, on the other hand, are much easier to photograph. If one creeps up carefully or lies patiently in wait one can get a magnificent photograph quite easily. Photographs of very tiny objects, such as very small insects, are usually taken by a technique

v

of micro-photography. These photographs are taken from a distance of some six inches or even less. With such methods one obtains very detailed photographs of the bodies of such insects.

In relation to animal photography, or for that matter any other photography, the sun is well worth discussing. On a grey, sunless day many details fade and disappear, swallowed up by the background, but on bright sunny days shapes and colours are thrown much more strongly into relief and become much more distinct.

This is about as much as one can mention in a brief note about the technique and ways of hunting with the camera.

It is very difficult indeed to discover all the secrets of photography from books alone, and just as it takes a good deal of practice to cook a good meal, so photography requires a good deal of practice as well a certain amount of theory.

In conclusion just let me say that, in common with a great deal of other work one needs a 'little bit of luck' when it comes to photography. Unfortunately I am not one of those 'very lucky' people. It seems that whenever I set out with my camera the sun immediately hides behind a cloud as if some unkind person had drawn a blind across a bright blue sky. I am, however, not very superstitious and this does not really put me out of countenance. I wait patiently for the sun and try to surmount any difficulties. In fact if it were not for this trait in my character this collection of animal portraits might never have come into being.

Author

GRAPHIC DESIGN

MATEUSZ GAWRYŚ

AND

HUBERT HILSCHER

PHOTOGRAPHY

WŁODZIMIERZ PUCHALSKI

BIRDS . . . . Page 1

REPTILES . . . . . . Page 65

MAMMALS . . . . . Page 73

Birdy

THE LONG EARED OWL.
A s i o   o t u s.

The long eared owl's eyes are surrounded by a very distinctive pink feathering. Note also the characteristic ruff of feathers. This owl lives in woodlands, forests and parklands.

The head of the owl is adorned with bristling feathers, and to some degree reminds one of a cat. The aperture of the ears is covered by a mobile semi-circular fold of skin.

The young long eared owl looks at the
camera with keen interest.

When in danger the owl bristles its feathers, and thus hopes to frighten away its enemies.

We are terrified! We try to make ourselves inconspicuous by having the same colouring as our surroundings.

THE TAWNY OWL.
S t r i x a l u c o.
This owl is one of the most frequently encountered species in Europe. It has a strong hooked beak, large black eyes and dark tawny brown or greyish feathers.

The young tawny owl is not at all dangerous, on the contrary he looks rather comical.

THE LITTLE OWL.
A t h e n e n o c t u a.
This is one of the smallest of our owls. It nests in dark recesses of lofts, towers, barns and other buildings.

It has a long drawn out call which can be very frightening, especially since owls are the subject of so much superstition, and seem to be universally regarded as birds of ill omen.

No rodent will succeed in escaping the sharp eyes of this little owl.

In the daytime he sleeps in the shade of trees and sets off to hunt at nightfall. He hunts rodents and small mammalia, but he is equally capable of carrying off a fully grown hare or a small doe, or even another bird larger than himself. His favourite titbit is the hedgehog, which he manages to catch quite easily despite the hedgehog's defensive spines.

THE EAGLE OWL. B u b o b u b o.
The eagle owl is sometimes called the "king of the owls" and he is the most dangerous of all the nocturnal birds of prey. Until quite recently he was to be found in the large, ancient forests of Europe, but today he is classed as a rare bird.

THE SEA EAGLE. Haliaetus albicilla. The sea eagle is the most magnificent though by no means the most dangerous of our European birds of prey. In the past it was found quite widely throughout Eastern Europe but is now a rather rare bird.

This is a young representative of this very beautiful species. A few tens of sea eagles can still be found in Western Poland along the Baltic coast and they are under special protection.

It has an extremely strong beak and it feeds chiefly on fish, water birds and smaller mammalia, but in times of starvation it will not scorn carrion.

THE GREAT SPOTTED EAGLE. *Aquila clanga.* This fledgling of the great spotted eagle is, despite its powerful looking hooked beak, still quite helpless. During the early period of its life it is covered by a thick, fluffy, white down.

This useful bird feeds primarily on mammalia, however, it sometimes feeds on reptiles and insects, and even on small birds.

The great spotted eagle is not much bigger than a hawk. It has beautiful chocolate brown plumage. It builds its eyrie in tall trees in the forests or woods where it lives.

THE GRIFFON VULTURE.
Gyps fulvus.

Even up to the middle of this century this bird was to be found on the Southern slopes of the Carpathians. Today it is becoming increasingly rare in Europe, but it is still to be found in some parts of Southern Europe.

The griffon vulture is a frequent "prisoner" behind the bars of zoological gardens. It stands captivity fairly well and does not cause any difficulties. It feeds mainly on carrion and that is why it is so useful in hot climates.

Vultures build their nests in crevices of rocks on steep, inaccessible rocky cliffs. Both parents take solicitous care of the young.

THE PEREGRINE
FALCON.
F a l c o p e r e g r i n u s.
The peregrine falcon is
today a very rare bird
throughout the world. It
lives in large forests and
in rocky, mountainous
areas of Central Europe.
It is very agile; it catches its quarry in full
flight and its amazing
speed allows it to catch
smaller mammals on the
move.

A characteristic feature of this falcon, in fact all falcons, is the curved beak and long pointed wings. The falcon has a notch in the upper mandible; this is a very recognisable feature. It frequently attacks much larger birds such as wild geese, herons or cranes.

In the past falcons were widely used in Europe for hunting. Today these birds are under protection in most countries.

THE KESTREL.
Falco tinnunculus.

This is the most common of the European falcons. It builds its nest in ruins and deserted towers and from time to time in the hollows of trees in woodland.

The kestrel feeds chiefly on mice and insects which it catches with great agility. It spots mice and such like from quite a height and plummets like a stone on them.

For this reason it is quite a useful bird
and is generally well protected.

THE HAWK. Accipiter gentilis.
This bird is the nightmare of pigeon keepers and fowl
breeders. One encounters it all over Europe. It likes to
occupy the nests of other birds of prey or crows.

The large orange coloured
eyes of the hawk have the
most dangerous glint in them.

The fledgling hawk.

THE FLEDGLING MARSH HARRIER.
Circus aeruginosus.
This fledgling marsh harrier looks as if he
is not enjoying this encounter with the
camera in the least. However, he is at the
moment very young and can do nothing but
adopt a defensive attitude.

During "babyhood" our dresses are white, light and warm...

The marsh harrier is a very common bird of prey and its nest can be found hidden deeply among the rushes on the banks of ponds and lakes.

It hunts for young reptiles, mammalia, waterfowl and toads. ▼

THE BUZZARD.
B u t e o   b u t e o.
The buzzard lives on the edge of forests, near the fields where it hunts for small rodents. As a rule it occupies large nests deserted by other birds.

The buzzard is one of the greatest allies of the farmer and the forester. It is as a rule fairly carefully protected.

THE RAVEN.
Corvus corax.
The raven is one of
largest members of the
crow family.

It is fairly widely found throughout Europe, but it is by no means
a common bird.

Its strong beak enables it to kill
with ease a young hare or even
a young doe. It feeds chiefly on
smaller mammalia, birds' eggs,
fledglings, grain and carrion. It
does not migrate.

ROOKS.

Corvus frugilegus.
Rooks are very gregarious birds and they build their nests in colonies in tall trees. They return to these nests each year.

Fledgling rook. ▼

The rook is one of Europe's most common birds and can be found at any time of the year in the countryside and even in the large cities. They are fairly useful birds since they feed on various noxious insects that are the enemies of the farmer. However, large colonies of rooks can do damage to crops and they have to be strictly controlled.

THE JACKDAW.
Coloeus monedula.
The jackdaw is a fairly common bird and is found throughout Europe. They live in hollow trees, often in the neigbourhood of rookeries, and in the crevices of buildings.

Young jackdaws can be easily tamed and are very intelligent.

THE TREE SPARROW.
Passer montanus.

The tree sparrow is the closest relative of the domestic or house sparrow. It resembles the house sparrow to a great degree and it is little wonder that it is just called a sparrow.

This is a fledgling tree sparrow that has only just recently left its nest.

Tree sparrows are generally quite entertaining with their gay twittering and they help to make the woods and forests more pleasant. They feed chiefly on seeds and grain but also help to rid the farmer of certain noxious insects.

THE RED BACKED
SHRIKE.
Lanius collurio.
This is the smallest
member of the common
shrike family.

He feeds on insects and lizards and even mice. He will
often kill his prey and impale it on the thorns of the
bushes where he usually prefers to live.

THE WAXWING. B o m b y c i l l a   g a r r u l u s.
The waxwing owes its name to the silky brown plumage
of its wings.

This beautiful bird is slightly larger than the sparrow and has exceptionally colourful feathers. During severe winters the waxwings move South from the distant North and return at the end of the cold season for the mating and hatching season. They feed on berries and fruit and, during the hatching season, on insects. Their favourite titbits are the succulent, coral-red service berries and the aromatic juniper berries.

THE BULL FINCH. P y r r h u l a p y r r h u l a.
Surely everyone knows this charming little bird,
with its brightly coloured plumage and cheerful
whistling song. This cheerful song adds a touch of
brightness to the parks and woodlands.

The bullfinch is quite a common bird throughout Europe.

Its strong beak enables it to split the thick husks of the seeds on which it feeds.

THE GREY PARTRIDGE.
P e r d i x p e r d i x.
The grey partridge is the most common of the semi-domestic gallinaceous species to be found in Europe.

In summer their plumage blends perfectly with their surroundings and even the sharp eyes of the hawk cannot discover them in the thickets of brushwood.

THE TURKISH
TURTLEDOVE.
Streptopelia
decaocto.
The turtledove came to
Europe quite recently
from the Far East.

It builds its nest with
small twigs preferably
in fruit trees.

This small and rather
beautiful pigeon is
more or less the same
size as the turtledove
that we all know.

THE MUTE SWAN. ▶
Cygnus olor.
This is one of the most
beautiful of our Euro-
pean aquatic birds.

The fledgling swans leave the nest almost immediately after they are hatched. They are excellent swimmers but when they tire of swimming they climb onto the backs of their parents for a ride.

The fledglings are covered with a silvery-grey down, they have short necks and very small legs, in fact they do not resemble their parents in the least during the early period of their life.

THE GREY LEG GOOSE.
Anser anser.
This is the ancestor of our domestic goose.

It nests in the dense reeds of large lakes. Once scared from the nest however, it hardly ever returns.

Portrait of a fledgling grey leg goose a few hours after having left its nest.

In case of danger the young gosling knows well enough how to hide itself away from the enemy's eye.

FLEDGLING
BLACK DUCK.
M y r o c a   f u l i g u l a.
This little fellow is as black
as if he were covered
with soot. He has brown
eyes and a light coloured
beak.

The black duck is a
representative of one of
the many species of duck
living in European waters.
It builds its nest in the
reeds of large and small
lakes.

▼

THE MALLARD. Anas platyrhynchas.
The plumage of the drake during the mating season is much more colourful than
that of the female.

A portrait of a female mallard. Its modest plumage permits it to camouflage itself easily when an enemy is near.

The drake mallard does not take very good care of his family. He never helps in the hatching and rearing of the young.

THE BLACK CORMORANT. Phalacrocorax carbo.
The black cormorant is found by the lakes and seashores of Eastern Europe.

The cormorants build their nests in tall trees close to the lakes where they feed.

Their diet consists chiefly of fish, for which they are able to dive deep into the water.

PORTRAIT
OF A FLEDGLING
BALDICOOT.
F u l i c a a t r a.

The baldicoot is today
quite a common bird
and is found in the
vicinity of small and
large lakes.

▼

THE GREAT CRESTED GREBE. P o d i c e p s   c r i s t a t u s.
This bird is widely found throughout Europe. It lives by lakes and
inland waterways and feeds chiefly on insects and crustacea for
which it dives.

PORTRAIT OF A YOUNG
HORNED GREBE.
Podiceps auritus.

The horned grebe is commonly found by all our lakes and ponds. It uses rotting weeds to build its nest. This nest is so cleverly attached to the reeds or bullrushes that the waves never carry it away.

This young "diver" spends most of his childhood days sitting on the back of his parents, when he falls off, as he sometimes does, they never fail to find him.

THE BLACK
HEADED GULL.
L a r u s
r i d i b u n d u s.
This gull is found
throughout Europe
especially during the
Spring migrations.

It is an excellent swimmer, runs very well and can remain in the air
for long stretches. In the autumn the gulls leave Northern Europe
and migrate for remote countries in the Southern hemisphere.

THE COMMON TERN. S t e r n a   h i r u n d o.
This bird is populary called the sea swallow, though
it has nothing in common with the swallow. It is an
aquatic bird and can be found anywhere where
there is an abundance of small fish.

The parents take care of their little ones in turn. The ash coloured feathers of the fledgling tern bear no resemblance to the white feathers of its parent.

The fledgling tern is able to swim with perfect ease only a few days after it is hatched.

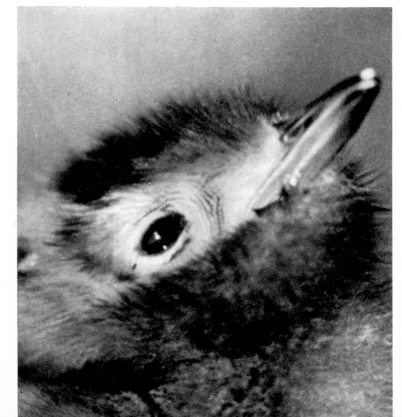

PORTRAIT
OF A YOUNG HERON.
A r d e a c i n e r e a.
The young heron will soon
leave its nest and fly
away in search of fresh
adventures.

Heron colonies can be
found throughout Europe.

The grey heron is found
on river banks and lake-
sides throughout Europe.
Here it can be seen wading
carefully among the reeds
hunting for food in the
early morning and at twi-
light.

When it is only a few hours old the fledgling crane is able to swim and walk very well. When young it is covered with a dense, rusty yellow down which renders it almost completely invisible to its enemies when in its natural surroundings.

THE CRANE. G r u s g r u s.
Portrait of a fledgling crane just a few hours old.

Due to the very wide span of its wings it is a very good flier and is able to glide for hours without even moving its wings.

THE WHITE STORK. Ciconia ciconia. This bird is quite widely known throughout Europe.

THE BLACK STORK. C i c o n i a   n i g r a.
Unlike the white stork this bird is very cautious and tends
to live in large forests. It does not enjoy man's company.

It eats the same sort of food as the white stork. This it catches in the woods and meadows.

It builds its nest in densely branched trees. Its fledglings are covered with white down and they do not resemble their parents until they are fully grown.

THE RUFF.
P h i l o m a c h u s p u g n a x.
The ruff is undoubtedly one of the most beautiful of our wading birds. It has a most original plumage.

▲

The females have a beautiful bright plumage and during the breeding season they grow a large ruff around the neck and ornamental tufts of feathers like ears.

They feed chiefly on insects, snails and rainworms which they catch in the meadows.

THE REDSHANK. Totaunus totaunus.
The redshank is found in meadowland and swampland
throughout Europe.

THE LAPWING OR PEWIT.
Vanellus vanellus.
The lapwing is one of the first harbingers
of Spring. ▶

The fledgling redshank leaves the nest almost immediately after hatching. Because of its protective plumage it can hide easily when danger is at hand.

Its long sharp beak enables it to find its food in the mud and wet slime of the fields.

Shortly after its arrival it lays about four brown speckled eggs in a temporary nest on the ground. After about three weeks of brooding the motley fledglings are hatched.

Young lapwings grow very quickly and after only a few weeks they are fully grown. In July they migrate in large flocks for the warmer countries of the South.

Portrait of a fledgling lapwing. The protective plumage makes it very difficult to spot, even in an open field.

Reptiles

THE EDIBLE FROG.
Rana esculenia.
This animal will lie for long periods, absolutely motionless, waiting for prey. When it sees a likely prey it will leap at lightning speed and catch it cleverly with the aid of its long, muscular tongue and well developed jaws.

During the mating season the males develop large "resonance balloons" and it is due to these that voice of the frogs can be heard from a great distance.

PORTRAIT
OF A COMMON
GRASS FROG.
Rana temporaria.
This inhabitant of the
meadows and fields is
very often the victim o
the stork.

In the early Spring the
frogs gather in shallow
water to mate. When
the eggs are laid the
frogs desert them and
scatter all over the fields
and meadows. They hi-
bernate in holes under
the roots of trees and in
ditches.

THE SWAMP FROG. Rana terrestris.
This frog is somewhat smaller than the edible frog. It lives for preference in wooded swamplands. It spends the mating season in small muddy pools and ponds. It is very cautious and not easy to find especially during the mating season. At this time the males develop a sky blue colour. In case of danger the frogs interrupt their mating and hide among the plants and slime at the bottom of the ponds.

THE TREE TOAD. Hyla arborea.
This toad lives among the bushes in forest and woodlands.
It feeds on small insects which it catches in mid air. It is
only found in the water during the Spring mating season.
At this time it deposits its eggs and departs. It does not
normally enjoy being in the water.

It is essentially a nocturnal animal and during the daytime it sleeps, hidden among the leaves. It wakes at twilight and sets out to hunt.

THE GRASS SNAKE. Natrix natrix.
This snake is perhaps the commonest
of all the European snakes. It is found
chiefly in damp woodland areas. It is
not venemous and never attacks or
bites people. It feeds on various insects,
but above all it likes frogs.

THE LIZARD. Lacerta agilis.
This is one of the most popular reptiles
of the woods and gardens.

Patiently and without a
movement it will lie in
wait for a passing insect
for hours.

It spends part of its life
hidden in burrows and
rocky crevices but in the
sunny weather it loves
to bask in the sun.

Mammals

THE OTTER. Lutra vulgaris.
This animal is quite widely found throughout Europe but despite the fact that it is a very cautious animal it is hunted down by fur poachers. This has been responsible for a marked decline in the European otter population. It seeks its food at nightfall. It eats in the water as a rule, but if it catches some rather large prey it will drag it to the shore and eat it there.

THE EUROPEAN MINK OR MARSH OTTER. Lutreola vison.

This creature is about half the size of the otter with an elongated, flattened body resembling a marten. Until quite recently it could be found here and there in rivers and lakes but it has unfortunately been almost completely exterminated and is only very rarely found in a wild state.

The European mink leads the same sort of life as the otter. It feeds mainly on fish, frogs, crustacea, insects and small birds.

THE WEASEL. Mustela nivalis.
The weasel is the smallest representative of the marten family. Its exceptional agility helps it to catch mice and other rodents.

The weasel lives in farm buildings, in burrows by the wayside and on the edges of woodland. Although it is quite a small animal it is nevertheless very aggressive and will attack and kill animals much larger than itself. It can, for example, easily kill a hare, rabbit or goose. Having murdered its victim the weasel sucks the blood from its throat and then leaves the carcase.

THE MARTEN. Martes martes.
This animal is popularly called the pine
marten. It differs from the other animals
of the weasel family in that it has a large
yellow patch on its breast. The beech
marten and other members of the family
have a white patch.

The pine marten has a very varied diet,
feeding chiefly on smaller mammals and
birds, insects, wild forest berries and even
eggs stolen from nests. Its favourite titbits,
however, are squirrels and honey.

It lives in large forests and
since it is primarily nocturnal it hides in the hollows
of trees during the day.

THE LYNX. L y n x l y n x.
This is the largest wild Central
European cat. It is perhaps
the most rapacious animal in
the forests.

THE WOLF. C a n i s l u p u s.
The wolf appears to be
growing in numbers in the
woodlands of Central and
North Eastern Europe. ▶

The lynx is subject to many stories and superstitions but, it is quite untrue that it attacks its victims by leaping at them from tall trees. It climbs such trees very rarely, and generally only when it is driven there by wolves or packs of hounds. It attacks roe deer, hares, does and birds. These it approaches silently and springs upon at the last moment.

The wolf is a dangerous animal and will attack sheep, calves, dogs and domestic fowl. In general, however, it prefers to hunt wild animals such as deer, stags and wild boar.

Despite its great rapacity it is a very timid animal. It will hide from man and it is very difficult to hunt because of its cautiousness.

THE FOX. Vulpes vulpes.
Everyone knows something of the fox,
the legendary hero of so many fairy
stories.

In autumn its fur blends perfectly with the browning leaves. This fur is much prized for its softness and fluffiness.

The fox lives in a burrow which it digs for itself among the roots of trees. Here it spends a great part of its life. The vixen usually has a litter of four to seven cubs which after a couple of days venture from the lair for short periods. However, they are quick to return if danger threatens.

THE BADGER.
Meles taxus.
The badger sleeps during the
day in subterranean burrows,
and ventures out only at night
in search of food.

Late in the autumn the badger
collects in its burrow a large
amount of dry leaves and
plants. He buries into the
specially prepared "bed"
and sleeps through the
winter.

THE BROWN BEAR. Ursus Arctos.

The brown bear was until quite recently a common inhabitant of the Central European forests, nowadays, however, it is rarely found here. It can still be found in certain parts as far West as the Tatra Mountains.

It lives mainly on berries, plants, insects and meat, but it will not scorn carrion. Its favourite titbit as most people well enough know is honey.

Late in the autumn the bears build their lairs in inaccessible places and hibernate for the winter. In December one to three cubs are born and these are very carefully guarded by their watchful mothers until they are about one year old.

THE COMMON HEDGEHOG.
E r i n a c e u s   e u r o p a e u s.
The hedgehog must be one
of the best known of all the
garden mammals. It makes its
appearance at night in the
gardens, parks and forests.

At twilight it sets out in search
of food. It eats primarily insects,
reptiles, amphibia and small
rodents. It will even eat the
fledglings and eggs of birds that
build their nests on the ground.

The hedgehog has many enemies despite its bristling armour
of spines. It frequently becomes
the prey of dogs and foxes.
It has one arch enemy, the eagle
owl. This bird considers the
hedgehog a particular delicacy.

THE DORMOUSE. D y r o m y s n i t e d u l a.
The dormouse is to be found primarily in beech woods. It hides in the hollows of old trees, and despite the fact that it is not at all uncommon, it is very difficult to find. It is primarily nocturnal and cautious.

It runs and jumps in trees with great agility. It feeds on seeds, fruit, berries and buds. It hibernates in a hollow or in deep burrows under the roots of trees.

THE SQUIRREL.
Sciurus vulgaris.
The squirrel is the real "balle[t] dancer" of the woods. It i[s] one of the few rodents tha[t] is not nocturnal. It lives i[n] the hollows of trees, but i[t] frequently builds nests tha[t] are made of twigs.

It eats seeds and fruit but fo[r] preference it will eat nuts.

THE MARMOT. Marmota marmota.
In certain mountainous regions in Eastern Europe one may be lucky enough to hear the warning whistle of the marmot. When an enemy approaches the marmot lets out a short sharp whistle that resounds through the valleys.

In the past, the marmot used to live in the lowlands, but the development and civilization of the lowland has driven it into the mountains.

It hibernates in burrows from which it emerges in the late spring, when the last snow has gone.

THE SPOTTED SOUSLIK
Citellus suslica.
This charming little creature can be found in certain parts of Central Europe. It is very agile and is rather like a miniature version of the dormouse.

It feeds on grass, grain and other seeds and when not kept down can be a nuisance to farmers. It hibernates in a burrow.

WATER VOLE
Arvicola terrestris
This small rodent is perhaps far better known as the water rat. It lives in the weeds by the river and lake side.

It is very cautious and so agile that it is not easily seen when it hides among the rushes. It moves with the same ease on both land and water.

THE HARE.

Lepus europaeus.

Few people will realize that the hare sleeps without closing its eyes. In fact this is exactly what the hare looks like when it is asleep.

A few days after having given birth to her leverets the mother leaves and the young are left to their own fate. It is not an easy life for them and they are often the victims of predatory animals.

The hare has many enemies — dogs, foxes, cats, birds of prey and above all man. No wonder therefore that the number of hares is decreasing year by year.

5

At present I do not resemble the wild boar in the least little bit. No wonder, I am only a few days old. I have a motley coat during my early days. This helps me to hide in the thickets of the wood.

THE WILD BOAR. Sus scrofa.
The wild boar feeds upon various plants, seeds, fruits, insects and meat. In the autumn it feeds chiefly upon hazel nuts and acorns.

The wild boar is the ancestor of the domestic pig and is a common inhabitant of the woods and forests of Central and Northern Europe. It likes the dense oak and beech forests.

EUROPEAN BISON. B i s o n b a n a s u s.
This animal was once quite common in the forests of Northern Europe. It was
hunted down and almost became extinct.

A few were however, specially bred in reservations in Poland and the species has been saved from final extinction.

THE RED DEER. Cervus elaphus.
The red deer is one of the most beautiful woodland animals.
It can still be found in Europe as a whole.

In the autumn the red deer has its mating, or rutting, season.
At this time the stags emit powerful roars as they challenge
their rivals to fight for the hind.

The hinds have no horns and are a little less magnificent than the stags.

THE ELK. A l c e s   a l c e s .
Elks are quite a rarity in Europe but there
are some to be found. They are much
more common in other parts of the world
such as America.

The antlers of the older elk have a marvellous broad palm-like expanse. They are really most magnificent.

he female elk, like the emale deer, does not arry any antlers.

THE ROE DEER. Capreolus capreolus.
The roe deer is widely distributed throughout the forests of Europe. If they were not so widely hunted by man they might be much more numerous. The female roe deer has no antlers.

The roe buck has magnificent antlers which serve primarily as a defensive weapon. Its antlers fall every year, late in the autumn and the new ones begin to grow within the first few months of the next year.

A young roe deer. There are not many animals that sit so well for their portrait.

The young roe deer has a protective colouring which makes it much easier for it to hide in the interplay of light and shade in the woodland.

THE BAT. Myotis myotis.
This bat is one of the most
common species. It is a most
useful animal.

Bats are completely noctu
nal in their habits. They slee
during the day, hangin
down from beams and niche
in cellars, garrets and dar
caverns.

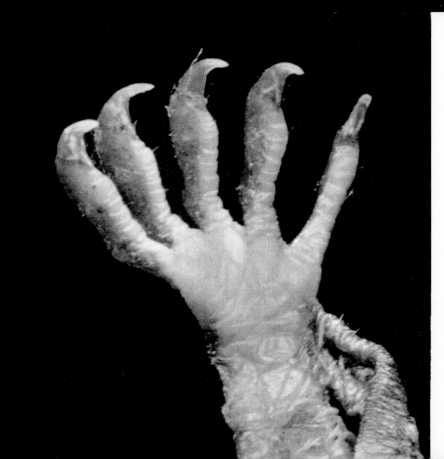

They have very sharp claw
on their hind legs, with th
aid of these they can easi
grip onto beams or roof

PORTRAIT OF A LONG
EARED BAT.
Plecotus auritus.

▶

In its sleep the long eared b
folds its ears and covers th
with its wings.

Bats hibernate in deep grottoes where the air is damp. Their body temperature drops to the same temperature as the surrounding air. They leave their hiding place in the spring.

THE HORSE SHOE BAT.
Rhindophus hipposideros.
This is the smallest of the European bats. Its ears have numerous notches and curves and these are adapted to receive very high frequency sounds. These are an indispensible part of the bat's navigational equipment.

During the winter when they hibernate they cover their bodies with their wings and they look somewhat like wizened hanging fruit.

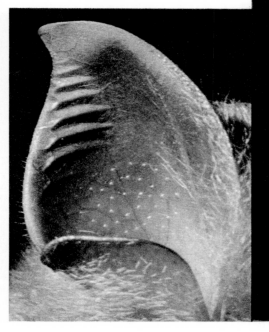

PRINTED IN POLAND
Drukarnia Narodowa w Krakowie